Whispers and Other Poems

Myra Cohn Livingston

Whispers and Other Poems

Illustrated by Jacqueline Chwast

Harcourt, Brace & World, Inc.

New York

D.6.67

Library of Congress Catalog Card Number: 58-5711

Printed in the United States of America by The Murray Printing Company

To Mother

Contents

WHISPERS

Whispers
    tickle through your ear
    telling things you like to hear.

Whispers
    are as soft as skin
    letting little words curl in.

Whispers
    come so they can blow
    secrets others never know.

JUST WATCH

Watch
    how high
      I'm jumping,

Watch
    how far
      I hop,

Watch
    how long
      I'm skipping,

Watch
    how fast
      I stop!

BUILDINGS

Buildings are a great surprise,
Every one's a different size.

Offices
grow
long
and
high,
tall
enough
to
touch
the
sky.

Houses seem
more like a box,
made of glue
and building blocks.

Every time you look, you see
Buildings shaped quite differently.

13

IN THE SAND

In the sand
A castle grows

    (ramps and towers, turrets, bowers, trees and flowers)
    and for hours
    kings and knights march through the land

    in between my toes.

TRAIN WINDOWS

Train windows always seem to be
Like picture frames for all I see—

> a painted sky,
> a running stream,
> or just a waving tree.

But when the train moves on so fast
My window pictures never last.

PICTURE PEOPLE

I like to peek
  inside a book
  where all the picture people look.

I like to peek
  at them and see
  if they are peeking back at me.

I KNOW A PLACE

I know a place
Where you turn on the hose
And take off your shoes
And wiggle your toes

    And the mud is oozy
    And sort of sloozy . . . .

(There's no one else who knows!)

THE MERRY-GO-ROUND

The merry-go-round
    whirls round and round
    in a giant circle on the ground.

And the horses run
    an exciting race
    while the wind blows music in your face.

Then the whole world spins
    to a colored tune
    but the ride is over much too soon.

THE BALLOON MAN

The balloon man's stall
Is near the wall.

And in the Spring
There's not a thing
In the afternoon
Like a bright balloon.

    (Big ones or small
    Round as a ball,
    Balloons with a string
    Or with nothing at all.)

He stands near the wall
In his bright-colored stall
And sells balloons
In the afternoons
In the Spring.

SLIDING

We can slide
   down
      the
        hill
  or
    down
       the
         stair
  or
    down
       the
         street
or anywhere.

Or down the roof
  where the shingles broke,
Or down the trunk
  of the back-yard oak.

Down
　　the
　　　　slide
　　　　　　or the ice
　　　　　　or the slippery street,

We can slide　　on our sled
　　　　　　or our skates
　　　　　　or our feet.

Oh, it's lots of fun to go outside
And slide
　　　　and slide
　　　　　　　and slide
　　　　　　　　　and slide.

THE DIFFERENCE

Outside
    the world is sky and air
    and trees and flowers everywhere.

But inside
    it is walls and floor
    that lead to outside through a door.

BALLOONS...BALLOONS

Balloons, balloons
    on colored string
    are blowing out
    into the Spring.

Balloons, balloons
    filled up with air
    are sailing off
    to everywhere.

Balloons, balloons
    all bright and round
    are floating up
    without a sound.

RAIN

Summer rain
    is soft and cool,
    so I go barefoot
    in a pool.

But winter rain
    is cold, and pours,
    so I must watch it
    from indoors.

AT THE ZOO

I've been to the zoo
 where the thing that you do
 is watching the things
 that the animals do—

 and watching
  the animals
  all watching

   you!

PRETENDING

When I put on my Mother's clothes
It seems my age just grows and grows,
And people think I'm quite sedate
Instead of being only eight.

When I dress up and curl my hair
I think I could go anywhere,
And be a lady at a ball
And never tell my age at all.

DISCOVERY

Round and round and round I spin,
Making a circle so I can fall in.

TAILS

A dog's tail
     is short
And a cat's tail
     is long,
And a horse has a tail
     that he
     swishes along,
And a fish has a tail
     that can
     help him
     to swim,
And a pig has a tail
     that looks
     curly on him.

All monkeys have tails
And the elephants too.

There are
hundreds of
tails
if
   you
      look
         in
           the
             zoo!

WINTER AND SUMMER

The winter
    is an ice-cream treat,
    all frosty white and cold to eat.

But summer
    is a lemonade
    of yellow sun and straw-cool shade.

MORNING

Everyone is tight asleep,
I think I'll sing a tune,
And if I sing it loud enough
I'll wake up someone—soon!

GROWING UP

When I am old and grow a bit
I think my Mother's clothes should fit.

And every one will stop to see
And wonder if it's really me.

CONFUSION

Tomorrow

      never seems to come.
      It will—they always say,
      But when you think it should be here
      It's turned into

              today!

MY OTHER NAME

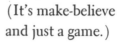

Jennifer's my other name
    (It's make-believe
    and just a game.)

·I'm really Anne,
But just the same
I'd much
    much
      rather
      have a name
      like Jennifer.

    (So, if you can
    don't call me Anne.)

NIGHT SONG

Out of the window
A yellow balloon
Is caught in the treetop
And looks like a moon.

Into the window
It smiles at me
And asks me to lift it
From out of the tree.

I DON'T KNOW WHY

I don't know why
    the sky is blue
    or why the raindrops
    splatter through

    or why the grass
    is wet with dew . . .   do you?

I don't know why
    the sun is round
    or why a seed grows
    in the ground

    or why the thunder
    makes a sound . . .   do you?

I don't know why
    the clouds are white
    or why the moon
    shines very bright

    or why the air
    turns black at night . . . do you?

COOKING

This will be a chocolate cake,
   This a cherry pie,
This will be a doughnut
   When the mud is dry.

PINCUSHION CACTUS

Right at the place
Where our garden begins
There's a cactus all covered
With needles and pins.

It's a very bright green
And as round as a ball,
And the pins and the needles
Are silver and tall.

But you have to be careful
Each time you go through
Or the cactus will prickle
Like pincushions do.

I FOUND

I found a four-leaf clover,
I put it in my shoe.
I thought my wishes over
And one of them came true.

OCTOBER MAGIC

I know
I saw
  a spooky witch
  out riding on her broom.
I know
I saw
  a goblin thing
  who's laughing in my room.

I think
  perhaps I saw a ghost
  who had a pumpkin face,
  and creepy cats
  and sleepy bats
  are hiding every place.

It doesn't matter where I look
There's something to be seen,

I know it is October
So I think it's Halloween.

FEET

Feet are very special things
For special kinds of fun.

On weekdays they walk off to school
Or skip—or hop—or run—

On Saturdays they roller-skate
Or bicycle—or hike—

On Sundays they just do the things
That other people like.

HEY DIDDLE

The cow is marked with spots of red,
Oh why can't they be blue instead?

If they were blue, I think that I
Would see her floating in the sky,

And clouds would be her hoofs and toes,
And one white puff her gentle nose,

And I would watch her jump, at noon,
Over the shadow of the moon.

THE NIGHT

The night
   creeps in
   around my head
   and snuggles down
   upon the bed,
   and makes lace pictures
   on the wall
   but doesn't say a word at all.

THOUGHT ON A STAR

A star
   is so far
   that it's very small
   and
   nobody . . .
   nothing . . .
   can touch it at all.

ALONE

Alone
> is when I'm tucked in bed
> and little things think in my head.

Alone
> is splashing out to meet
> the ocean waves beneath my feet.

Alone
> is in the apple tree
> with no one looking up at me.

THE MOURNING DOVE

The mourning dove has built a nest
Up where the latticework is best.

With twigs and leaves and bits of string
The nest is made of everything.

And in the nest, down deep inside
Two tiny speckled bird eggs hide.

And while she sits and softly sings
The mother shields them with her wings.

And coos and calls with mourning words
And warms her little unhatched birds.

BACK-YARD SWING

High up, high
    in the back-yard swing,
    listen to the summer wind,
    listen to it sing.